T0077874

POETRY FOR THE LOST SOUL

JEFFREY CARLTON

authorHOUSE

AuthorHouse™
1663 Liberty Drive
Bloomington, IN 47403
www.authorhouse.com
Phone: 833-262-8899

Published by AuthorHouse 06/14/2022

ISBN: 978-1-6655-6244-7 (sc)
ISBN: 978-1-6655-6245-4 (e)

Library of Congress Control Number: 2022911174

CONTENTS

PREFACE

Poetry for the Lost Soul is a collection of thoughts and ideas I have written over a thirty year period while attempting to struggle through a number of different and major transition periods in my life – that of saying goodbye to my youth while endeavoring, with much reluctance, to pass through the remaining decades of my life. I also found myself working through the death of my sisters, one of leukemia the other of cystic fibrosis, and soon after a girlfriend who died from cancer while finally, a father who passed away in my arms.

As you may have deduced, the works herein were written in an attempt to help all those people who, like me, have found themselves in or perhaps approaching, transition stages in their lives. This may include junior high school students trying to survive those turbulent years of high school, growing from young punks into young adults; high school students trying to assimilate themselves into that "college of their choice," readying themselves for entry into what is so unfortunately yet pretty much accurately called the "cold, cruel world."

They are also for married people who suddenly find themselves caught up in bitter divorces, now wondering where, how, why, what they did wrong. And also for people with loved ones so dear to them who might be dying, who might be dead...when God, for some reason, needed them more than they ever could have, despite the love. And they ask now, "What have we done to deserve this?"

This collection of poems and essays does not serve to answer any questions or doubts, nor does it guarantee absolution of any unnecessary guilt. They exist only to let the reader know that there has been at least one other person who has traveled the same journey, taken the same paths, asked the same questions, and been haunted with those same nagging doubts and that same obsessive guilt. These words were written so that all who read them will know that this person has survived and now knows – is now able to say – that simply being alive in this world of anguish, being able to live through the pain of each ordeal encountered, makes everything...no, makes all things...worthwhile!

On these pages do I write about the loneliness of children and the pain of adolescence. I also acknowledge the presence of a painful emptiness that can come about with each stage of the growth and development of one's life – the unfortunate need to leave behind certain childhood dreams – allowing a balm of maturity to thus overwhelm.

I have written about the fallibility of the human condition, of mistakes and their consequences, and of the sometimes futile attempts at second chances. And I have written about an even more painful discovery – that in this mortal world of ours, in these, our quiet, desperate lives, there do truly exist unrightable wrongs.

I have also counseled the wisdom of the ages in an attempt to better understand time – not only as a constructive healer but also as an incredulous witness to the erosion of all man-made creations.

Jeffrey A. Carlton

An Angel's Descent

Kaleidoscopic images of an angel gone down
Down...
Ever always down.
Overwhelmed completely
By a dark and indefatigable
Abyss of wondrous delights.

Fearful bloodied vultures
On wings of blackened souls
Swirling 'round the midnight skies,
Circling overhead;
Circling as they fly;

Ever always searching...
Searching for the angel,
That angel gone down,
Down...
Ever always...
Down.

And So Shall it always be

A man without reason, no causes to die for...
A man with no spirit, no soul there to live for...
Cries for his true love, who never existed,
And cries for his lost soul, a soul long tormented.
Damned to the sultry, sunbleached fires of Hell,
Driven to madness in a flow'ry dell.

I cannot cry for the unicorn, so long lost, forlorn,
Nor mourn for Adonis, immortals unborn,
For God, in His wisdom, kindness and joy,
Has given to us a new baby boy;
To be King of all kings, Lord of all lords;
To reign over us all, a reign without swords;
Who will die for each and all of us,
And leave us to carry his words.

And We as Mountains

Mountains soaring, sleek, majestic,
Undaunted in their stoic pleasure
While avoiding all the daily hectic
Pressures which we use to measure
Our day in, day out apophatic
Life and death we seem so to treasure.
God in Heaven, Lord on High,
We to you come to glorify,
And in Thy Presence so magnified,
Save you to us please thus sanctify.

The Apprehension of a Life Lost

I sit here, wond'ring where it's gone,
This life of sixty years,
Where has it gone?
If anything of meaning has occurred,
I can't recall,
That is to say, I really can't recall.

And as I sit here, waiting...
Thinking...
Wondering...
Waiting for the blackness of death to consume me...
Thinking that it is surely taking its time,
And wond'ring if thoughts such as these
Merit the importance I have been giving them,
It comes to me, suddenly – a flashing realization,
That this life of mine, these three score years,
Have here in waiting all been spent to die...

And now, while still alive, still wond'ring why...
Why...for wanting all to end,
Only to have it not...
Only to have looked for all...
All...
For naught.

But For Death, How Would We End?

The time draws near, our time to die. In the air I feel it coming as I stop to watch the people running, as if its shadow, its grasp, its presence, were merely fleeting, illusory wisps of incorporeal vapors, and thus by the foot, escapable.

O fervent fools are they, to believe this day might never come, or when it did, that it just might pass them by. How could they forget that in owning life, they need also own up to the inevitable, their ensuing death?

Yet, what is death, that they need fear it so? Is just another life, another start. Simply put a new beginning. Another journey down a different path, turning left at the fork in the road where earlier they had once turned right. Just another journey, with a different beginning and a different ending as well, sometimes better and other times worse, but really, on the whole, not that different from the road currently traveled. But that their present destination and final journey's end will differ, the two paths are really quite similar, and both are of equal importance, the one always necessary to the other. For without the life and the living, what reason have we to mourn the dead? And without this death, what cause have we to celebrate the life?

Death is not to be perversely sought after or longed for, yet neither is it something to be feared. It's presence in the universe is as obliquely natural as both yours and mine. So know, when it does come, it is to be embraced and welcomed, because when all is said and done, without it, without an end in our lives somewhere, how could we go on?

Can You Hear the Gods Cry?

There upon the blood-washed sands of Ebben-tree,
Near the snowcapped mountains rising from the sea,
The gracious, fragile winterflowers take their stand
Against the windswept caverns there at Sonnet-Lea.

Sonnet-Lea, it's oft been said,
Has never given up her dead;
For as the wars of Montezuma raged,
Their villages in ruins,
Their temples there ablaze,
The gods looked down with a tearful gaze,
And with mournful hearts and broken souls,
Cried out, "O my children, how couldst be so?
"Alas, how couldst be so?"

But still the warriors battled on,
Taking no captives, allowing no calm;
Until finally, on one bright and sunny morn,
On one much too quiet a dawn,
The lifeless, quiet bodies lay there, scattered anon
Amidst the gracious, fragile winterflowers,
The only things on this early dawn...
The only things left...
To carry on.

The Children's Hour
A Trilogy

Part I

Cry the unborn children,
Voices in the night;
Fie to those who wouldn't save them
And fie to those who wouldn't try.
Damn the world for its feigned abhorrence,
Damn the world to shame,
But die, the unborn children,
Their souls all damned to Hell.

Part II

All the little children,
Standing straight and tall;
Some are fat, some are thin,
God's little acre, all.
Some defy us, some deny us,
Some carry us along;
Some excuse us, some bemuse us,
All doing right and wrong...
All the little children,
God's little acre, all.

Part III

Suffer the lonely children,
Suffer one and all...
Belie the lonely children,
Deaf ears turned to them all...
Deny the lonely children,
Deny them one and all...
Cry the lonely children,
Guilt and despair to them all...
But they'll die, you know, they will,
All those lonely children...
With hearts full of love unborn.

The Children's Hour, Continued

Children, naked in the street
are dying,
dying slowly...

Maggots, feasting at their feet,
are chewing,
chewing slowly...

Mothers, with them, are too weak,
can't help them,
can't help them at all...

Water, bloody, in the sink
is draining,
draining slowly...

The Cost of Freedom Most True

Once...
On a journey through the naked emptiness of time,
Thru the land of quiet, shadowed dreams,
At that moment when the vast expanse of loneliness
Greeted the eternal wonders of being free,
I found myself lost, alone, and wondering why...
Why so lost...
  Why so alone...
    Why so wondering why...

I was beyond the emptiness,
I was past the dreams,
I had made it through the loneliness,
I had arrived to enjoy being free;

And I was free now,
Yet still was I lost...
Still so alone...
And still full of wonderment,
Still wondering why...

The promise of freedom,
Of a wealth beyond dreams,
Would allow, they promised,
A life such as only the gods had seen!

But still I was alone here,
By myself, quite alone,
And I am quite human,

Am here, a mortal, unknown...
And this life here, this freedom,
This freedom beyond dreams,
This life without emptiness,
What does it really mean?

It has become here a feeling
Most hollow and bare;
It was not fought for, It was unearned
And was bought, like a street whore,
By myself, unconcerned
With its value and meaning,
Its true reason for being,
As though I could get to Heaven
By merely purchasing train fare.

I have found I cannot possess
This notion of freedom,
Without needing the shadows,
Without dreaming the dreams,
And finally, without expecting some loneliness
To bump into my schemes;
It's a belief all-inclusive of each of these things.

It is a concept where life, death, war and peace, love, hate, pride and prejudice,
laughter, tears and loneliness, emptiness and dreams and their fulfillment all
come together to give me glorious reasons to know why I want to be alive or
why I want to be dead, and it gives me the glorious ability and freedom to
choose the path I truly desire.

The Day the Stone Rolled Away

On feathered wings of exquisite design,
Over turbulent seas of soylent green,
Amassed a thunderous clamor of hearts benign
That declared a love and peace set free.

On wings of fire thus didst come
That rage of Paradise, Homeward bound;
With passions so grand they 'clipsed the sun
With desires so fierce didst Heaven resound.

And found on the tips of their silken plumage,
There, to grace those wings of virgin snow,
Were brilliant diamonds placed in homage;
Homage to the stone which that day didst roll.

It was rolled away that day,
You see, that day it rolled away;
For then did God summon forth His Heavenly gathering
To return to Him His son;
To dispatch with haste, without delay...
To give us back the light,
And with it...
Our glorious reason for being...
For he has come home now,
And we have been saved.

A Discourse on Death and Dying

There is a time for death,
A reason for its existence.
It is a time for all men to depart,
Leaving behind all that was theirs,
Both of the flesh
And of the heart.
It is a calling of sorts,
A demanding of presence;
To give an accounting
Of unfulfilled promises,
Of broken dreams,
Of still-born desires.
It is a time beyond all reasoning
An ultra-dimensional detention of the soul, if you will,
That once accomplished, offers no reward...

              No pleasure...

                  No lift to the spirit;

Only a sense of completion;
Only the gifted knowledge
Of a full circle
Finally complete.

Emmanuel, Come to save us

I

O come, o come, Emmanuel,
To Beth'lem come Emanuel,
To save us here, to save from hell
Our souls...
Our dying, frightf'lly crippled souls

II

Please hear, o Lord, our feeble cries,
Our wretched moans, our mournful sighs,
And bring us home, we pray, to die;
To die for you...
For you our sins a-tolled.

III

And if to Heaven we might ascend,
If to Your throne we might attend
We'll kneel with grateful wonderment;
And then to You and to Your son,
We shall with greatness then extol.

The Emptiness of a Self-Imposed Silence

Perched precariously here
On this ever trembling,
Always threatening
Branch of my desire
On this ever crumbling tree of this my life,
I watch as below me
Two lumberjacks with malicious intent
Do cut away with their blades of sharpened steel
At the foundation of my life,
Doing their all to sever me
From the capstone of this,
My corporeal being.

My pleas for them to cease,
Coupled with threats of unspeakable redress
Should they not,
Remain unheeded, unanswered,
Fallen as they have
Upon the deafened ears and disquietous hearts
Of bloodsucking leeches.

Silence now...
A chilling echo of caustic silence
Does greet me now as I find myself drowning
In this blackened sea of unrepentant sins...
Unrequited loves...
Unanswered prayers...

Conceiving itself in fashion
By the deafening cries and maddening desires

Of so many empty, hollow hearts;
Each of them, all of them
Stopping...
So very suddenly stopping.

And the pain of such loneliness, this grief
Crying out in the night,
Adds its silence to mine,
Creating ever new rooms of dying tranquility,
Soon to be rented out or leased
As a final resting place for solitude,
A solitude in scent-surround,
Scented therein with the sights and sounds
Of a thousand crippled souls.

Entreaty for a New Beginning

Teardrops falling,
Silently...
Slowly...
Like a silver mist of dew
Over a countenance of rare beauty.

I saw them, I say
I saw them, and
I'm sorry and
dying inside
Because I caused them,
I know
I caused them.

Help me, please, to help you,
Show me, please, what I should do.
For above all else, please know
I do love you
and I am truly sorry.

Epitaph for a Mouse

A mouse is in the trap
He's dying
Can't you hear him calling out
He's crying
See his children come to him
They're crying
Why it wasn't one of them
There dying

Eternally Yours, J.C.

Inner space, outer time,
Exacting rhythm without the rhyme.
The gnarled creatures in horrendous pain
Watch, as a tasty ginger man writhing headlessly
Remains atop the bounteous,
Ornamental tree so grand,
Giving life to a babe,
An eternal concept to man

Eulogy for Scott

Sitting on a chair, crouched over,
His heartbeats slowing...slowing...stopping.
Holy, wholly empty heart,
He had no chance,
No chance from the start.
His face bleach white,
Turning whiter ever still;
Lips of purple, dark shades of crimson,
If you must, death, come you will,
And as you must to all of us,
Death, come you did for our friend Scott.
God speed, blithe child,
Take care of our son.

Far Away in Times of Valor

Far away, in dreams unfathomed,
Far beyond the gods' domain,
There dwells an evil, murderous phantom,
A force quite monstrous and gnarled with pain.

It plans a journey, this very night,
One through time and space forgotten;
It's coming home, coming here to this site,
We must make haste and prepare for the fight.
For its demonic illusions of universal conquest
Must not be taken light,
This is an evil, monstrous power obsessed
With the destruction of all in its sight.

So quickly, quickly, take heed what I say,
Not a moment to lose, dear friends,
There's no time for delay.
You must gather your children
And place them secure
In your homes, in your towns,
Anywhere to be sure
That the barbaric fiend will not hunt them down,
Will not chew them to pieces,
Will not swallow them down
Into the acids and oils known to exist
In the belly of the beast,
Most acrid and foul.

And those daughters you have, untouched by mankind,
You must hide from this demon,
This creature of slime!
As for you, all the rest, watch out for yourselves,
Retreat to your basements,
Hide out on your shelves.
Anything, anything, just do what you must,
The moment is near, the creature upon us.

And I and my men, most valiant and brave,
Will remain to protect you,
To ward off the knave.

Lo!
In the sky!
In the east, coming 'round,
Its ship bold and brilliant, spiraling down.
And there, I should say, 'most three miles away,
Will we lie in wait, hiding,
To ambush and slave.

So upward and onward men,
Come, follow me!
To save here these people,
To help them free.
And as for ourselves,
A most memorable fight –
One we must win!
One we must right!

And all here will tell
Of our glory this night,
When evil had tried
With its twisted might,
To kill off all good,
To kill all that was right
And then lost...
Destroying only itself in the fight!

For Anna, Forever My Love,
Forever My Saving Gracc

O Anna, my love, my sweet joyous love,
Each time I awake and see you lying here beside me,
I give thanks to the Lord
For bringing you so gently into my life.

My dear, beloved Anna,
Know my love for thee is infinite,
For you have always been there for me,
With your gentle strength and quiet tenderness
Offering me solace and protection
In the comfort and security of your warm embrace.

I remember when first we met,
It was during the darkest time of my life,
When blackness threatened to consume my soul;
It was then you came to me and, sensing my pain,
Didn't you chase the clouds away
And cause the sun to shine once more.

So for it all I give you thanks,
For the strength, for the will,
And for all your love...
That love given me at a time of greatest need,
Allowing me then to leave behind a once wretched life...
Allowing me then to find a peace of mind...
Allowing me then to find once more,
A reason for living.

For Esther, Wherever I May Find Her

I dream of Esther
When she pesters
The hell out of me;
She is an angel from heaven,
Come here to save me?
Without her my soul,
It cries;
It withers, it crumbles,
It dies.
And then she comes back to me,
And then she is mine;
And when we're together,
Both she and I,
Then we are fine.

Forever My God with Thee

Overwhelmed as I am by the cold, dark earth around me I fear this death of mine has finally come. Yet in this darkness, in the absolute, everlasting, empty blackness, I have found for my soul a peace, a truly placid serenity, the likes of which I, as a person once of this earth, did never know.

How cruel and unfair this is, this death, that it should allow only here, only now, for my soul, my spirit, to be blessed with this true peace, this utterly fortuitous tranquility. For in this spirit world, this abyss of incorporeal cosmic dust, though I find myself so completely freed from all earthly shape and form, it is yet still in this freedom where I have also found certain restraints – restraints that do continually deny any physical pleasure from this freedom and thus thwart my every effort to, even for the briefest moment, receive any sort of personal gratification from this serenity in which I find myself so rudely thrust.

Interestingly though, as an aside, I have found that this constant thought of self, the sudden recognition of individual rights and pursuits of pleasures does, as I lie here in this dark, hollow pit of despair, despair me not. For in this peace and with this limited freedom, I do find myself gradually coming to terms with this death. And with this understanding has come an acceptance that my soul, in the truest sense, is finally at peace, my spirit finally at rest. And I...now here, forever with my God, I am finally happy...and alive.

Forever My Love, Forever My Cherished Wife

A love most cherished, so dear to my heart,
These five and fifty years beside me, my wife;
With a love so powerful ne'er could I fall
From her heart, from her arms, from her grace; ne'er at all...
A love strong and pure, by god twas ordained,
To give life to my soul, my soul once untamed.
She gave me my everything, my need to survive,
My desire to live, a purpose most high.

But she's gone away now, left me lost and alone,
Taking with her my spirit, cutting quick to the bone.
And now, on these cold, lonely nights have I spent here in sorrow
As tears of my grief I have shed and will continue to shed
Long past the morrow.

But this I do know,
That the time will soon come for me to move on,
To carry on with my life, maybe sing a sad song;
To climb out of my anguish and do away with my strife...
And then armed with the memories of a love most benign,
Those five and fifty years with this woman, my wife
Will carry me onward, endow me with strength
And a knowledge secure,
That for a brief time – only a moment for sure,
I shared a life with my true love...
A life and a love God allowed to endure.

For Nidia, My Love of Centuries Past

The dust of a civilization long past
Filters down through my nostrils
And creates there amidst the cosmos of my being
A lustful, wanton need of resurgence,
A tremendous desire to be reborn.

For having died once already,
And then perhaps, to be given this second chance...
To be thus rewarded,
To be so divinely favored,
Would lift up my once conquered soul in offering,
And, as manna to my ascending spirit,
Breathe a new life into my ephemeral being.

But new beginnings are not easily come by,
Not for mortals or immortals alike;
Not in this...
Not in any lifetime.

This is not to say they are never attainable,
Rather, only that the rarity of such a gift
Would be the rule, and not the exception.

So if ever you might find yourself
Presented with such a glorious, blessed endowment,
Do not refuse, as did I...
                    Do not reject, as did I...
Is there but for the taking.

So then, in the aftermath of an act most foul,
When perhaps a scene of revilement was acted out,
A scene of inane reprehensity...
Something most desired to recant...
Something most desired to atone for...
To make amends for...
Do not hesitate, as did I...
Otherwise you may find the moment gone...
The sun to have already set...
And that part of your life,
Dead...
Run into a brick wall,
To an end...
      To a miserable...
            Stupid...
                 Damnable...
                     End!

At that point, reach out!
Just reach out
And grab that offering with swiftest grace...
Risking life, limb
And yes...
Even soul.
Just get down on your knees
To try...
To try once more...
To get it right.

So then for you, o Nidia,
My love of centuries past;
For you, my love,
Should you ever return,
Please know, that this time,
Yes, this time...
Please know...
It will be done right!

For Sarah, an Unspoken Truth, a Time to Speak

I have always thought you had known how I feel,
But if perhaps mistaken, I'll tell you now,
With hopes that soon these thoughts of mine
For you will become quite real.

That come each dawn, I gaze upon you lying there
With your locks of gold that flow so long,
It's just, my love, you make me feel so wanted,
You make me feel so strong;
Indeed, you make me feel for all the world to see
That finally do I belong.

For deep within those eyes of darkest blue
Have I there seen that you are someone
So very, very special to me;
Someone who is gentle, yet strong,
And someone who will be there for me
To fight for what is right
And put straight all wrong.

So please know that I need you,
I want you to be my love;
For in this, my quiet, desperate life
There's no one higher above...
None needed nor more precious to me...
None do I adore more than thee...
My quiet, my tender, my Ladylove

And this I do swear,
That should e'er your mind in troubled anguish be,
Know that I will be there to protect you,
And that I will stay there with you until trouble's end;
For I had been once before at that same place myself;
And my once ravished heart, with all its scars revealed,
Will be there, opened to you,
This love given unconditionally...
For all time.

So know my truth and come with me,
For with my heart and with my all,
Shall I love and cherish you.
And with your love added thence to mine
We will together Paradise find
And will, through our love, truly live divine.

Hobos, Heroes and Street Corner Clowns

There's a man on our block,
Says he's been everywhere...
From Egypt to China
And back again;
To Greenland and Iceland
And Hawaii too;
Even the North Pole
And the South Pole, he says.
He's been describin' the people,
Their habits and stuff.
My father says he's just fibbin',
Just lyin' to us all;
That they are all tall tales
He dreams up
While he travels around the world
On a map...
     On a wall...
         In his house...
             On our block...
                On the street corner...
                    Where he lives.

Home Can I Call Thee?

Midnight sunstorms, winds of fire,
A passion for dying, a most wanton desire.
When though I call thee, I hear no response;
Passions' flames come a-rising, come rise to engulf us.
Here ye, hear me, come list whilst I lie here,
Struggling against hopes most perverse that I die here.
O, per chance to sleep in the trees in the glen;
I am so lonesome, so tired, so lost my old friend.
For seventy years I have wondered alone,
From land to land...
                From sea to sea...
                        From home to home...
O God, for a resting place to call my own.
What I would give to thee,
What could I give to thee...
My love I will give to thee
My love everlasting, my love there to see;
O God, for a resting place to call my own.

I Will Die No More – Forever!

As I stood there studying the fetid corpse at my feet
While wondering at the manner and the cause of its defeat,
I gazed at the hideous disfigurement of its life-force,
That vile disembowelment of his soul, which in due course
I found did bring to me with painful inflection,
A smile of gleeful, sadistic abjection.

For 'twas then I noticed the broken shards of glass,
Carelessly, senselessly, strewn about the bloodied grass;
And a knife with a blade of rusted steel
Lying, streaked in vermillion, at my heels.
These clues did suggest to me a psychopath
With a wanton, insatiable thirst;
Indeed, a thirst and an appetite
Of horrendous delights, that at first
Inflamed my soul with an anger so grand
That it threatened my own life-force,
The very meaning of who I am.
And the feeling of such an undermining impotence,
That overwhelming of my soul,
Did near to pull me under...
                    Consume entirely...
                            Eradicate in whole.

But my spirit, though drained,
Called painfully for withdrawal,
For my feet to high-step it and run for cover
Away from that hellhole;
To forget all that I'd seen there

And run, run into the night,
To leave behind that fiendish nightmare
And steal away from that ungodly sight.

So then, in that time of unexpected clarity,
My soul, spirit, will and feet from there,
In oneness and with all alacrity,
Did ride the wind in a desperate yet vital quest
For my freedom, and with luck, a new life,
A life filled with zest.

Yet cursed there did I seem to be,
Despised by my God and His Son, and then finally
Abandoned by all...
All hope there inside me,
Gone...
Returned to ashes, vanquished, set free;
And all those so dear to me,
Each one a part of me,
Gone...
Still so very much now,
Gone...

And in that moment of quiet desperation,
While passing through that
Never-never land of unholy schemes
Did I find, running as I was
Into the fields of stillborn dreams,
The answers to all questions – a quenching of my thirst,
And a gift of spiritual freedom
I'd been seeking since my birth.

For then did I see, looking back again,
That lump of rotted flesh lying there, consumed with maggots,
Suddenly awaken and in a decadent splendor rise
With hopes of tearing me down once more,
Seeking again my demise,
Only to find, to its surprise,

Only to find – too late, it realized,
That my spirit, once conquered,
My soul, once defeated,
Would not, in its steadfast refusal,
Permit this crime to occur once again,
Would not again accept defeat, for sure.

So then did I cease my running,
And there did I take my stand,
To search the endless folds of maggots,
Crushing all that I found
In the hollow emptiness of my hand;
And then, looking upon this nameless evil
While fighting my way through this blackened death
Did I, with a new-found inner love for life
Strike down with a purity of heart
And smite its ne'er existent soul,
To send it crashing down straight-way
Into the blazing fires of Hell,
That Hell from whence it came, I'm told.

For indeed I tell you,
As long as the blue skies surround me
And the grass grows green at my feet,
I swear to you, my children,
I will die no more...
Forever!

The Importance of Time Wisely Spent

There is a time for the procreation of human souls;
That is, there comes a time when, at last,
There is a time for life,
For living...
Indeed, there is a time when a time will come
For loving...
      For living...
            For laughing...
                  For wanting...
                        For crying...
And tho few desire to speak of this,
There will come a time when, at last,
The time comes for the cessation of life...
For dying.

All of these events will occur
At least once in the course
Of a person's lifetime;
It is as inevitable as the passage of time itself.
And since no person has any control
Over when each of these events might take place,
And since, but for birth and death,
We have no idea whether they will ever occur again,
It becomes our responsibility to decide
How to react to each given experience.

Will we anguish over freedoms lost
On that fateful day of matrimonial bliss,
Or instead see days of wondrous happiness
At the prospect of sharing a love and a life with another?

It is also up to us to determine the length and intensity
Of each new emotion or experience endured;
Will we allow an event of great happiness
To be forgotten in a day's time?
Or perhaps take an event of unbelievable anguish
Unforgotten...
To the grave.

However each of us chooses to respond,
It will be our final decisions,
Our decisive reactions,
Which, in the final analysis,
Will all come together
To build and finally mold
The character of each of us...
And in the end,
The character of our society.

The Inevitable Destiny of Evil Most Foul

Crimson teardrops fallen upon a satin sheet of snow
Lead me on my quest...
Tell me in which direction to go.
Not much further ahead is he,
I can smell his fear;
In fact the stench of his death
Becomes worse as I near.
The atrocity of his crimes,
So perversely erotic in design,
Bespeak a cruelly twisted and angry mind,
A sort of genius at play
With a touch of puzzling wonderment
At who could really mind...
Who, indeed, should really mind?
An animal, tho, is all he truly is
A brilliant savage, wild and loose;
And I will do what all that I must
To hunt him down and capture him,
Then prepare him for the noose
That is awaiting him at the end of the trail...
At the end of a rope...
       At the end of his life...
           At the beginning...
               Of his death.

The Infinite Bewilderment of Loneliness

Psychedelic illusions of momentary madness,
Like dreams on the half-shell,
Intertwine and interfere with my conscious desires.
The metamorphosis, now complete, has thus
Disguised – aborted, if you will, my soul,
From the once ephemeral being
That was my master and my god.
Oh yes, to be free,
To be so completely free,
And yet so alone...
So very much alone now.
The basking, the reveling of
Such a contemptuous mindset...
Never hated, never hating,
O glory!
Never loved, never loving,
O the pain!
It hurts so much I wish to die!
O silly boy!
O silly thought!
To be free to die?
O silly boy!
To be free to live!
To live an eternal life?
O silly thought!
O god, please...
Help...
Help me...

Help me dream...
Help me dream to live...
To live with you...
For you...
For us.

In Life and Death, a Search for True Meaning

Cast adrift in the silence and solitude found in this drowning pool of quiet, empty souls, I find myself in a desperate need and frantic search for a life beyond this vortex, an existence across this void of unearthly passions.

This life of mine is so empty, so hollow in its meaning and so desperate in its need – would that I could die to end it all, I would indeed! But death is only another door to a different realm, and there would I enter with yet all the baggage I now claim – the same problems, the same trials, the same woes, still unresolved and still there to torment me further.

What then is the answer? What then might I do to escape this dilemma in which I find myself, this ledge I straddle, overlooking a bottomless pit I dare not think to fall into, no matter how desirous and enticing such a thought might seem.

Is all so lonely here, so very quiet and so very alone. But in this solitude, my heart does tell me, will I find my strength, my saving grace. It will only come once I seek out my peace – my peace with mankind, my peace with nature, my peace with a universe forever unfolding, my peace with my soul, then finally, with my God. When this is accomplished, then and only then will my anxieties, like the walls of Jericho in days of old, crumble to lay around me in worthless pieces, insignificant without their sense of cohesive unity and wholeness.

I know it will happen. That my mind, my heart and my soul will, in this emptiness, find this peace, this need to continue, this strength and desire to carry on. No matter how lonely, how painful the journey, I must push myself to want to go on until I finally discover this peace I desire.

Yet perhaps I might fail, even after forever journeying forward as far as both physical and spiritual forces would allow. Even then, however, should I fail, I will be at peace with the knowledge that I did, at least, attempt to find that happiness and for a time put aside those haunting troubles that have besieged me.

Once realizing this, a glow of satisfaction, of pride, of accomplishment has been instilled in my being. This belief that I did all that I could, attempted all that was feasible, and strove ever onward until that coming day when death does stand before me. It will then forever please me to know that this time it is my God's desire to have me...His desire to bring me into His light, and not my selfish, petty need to be with Him, there in the darkness.

Invitation to Beauty

Gazing upon a distant star of mystical, opulent elegance;
Indeed, a dazzlingly glorious sensation,
The most beauteous by far of all God's creation.
Brilliant and bold,
Unyieldingly cold,
Mysterious in every appearance;
Wonderingly, maddeningly she calls to me,
Effervescently daring an answer;
Every night to me like this she speaks,
Each spell of darkness a crying out,
Won't I somehow, in some manner, commune,
And acknowledge her existence.
Yet still from me does silence stir
Tho in truth an awestruck whisper,
Which does not reach her out-stretched ears,
Nor dissipate her growing fears.
Canst do no more, not at this time,
I can find no rhythm without first the rhyme;
Finding first the reason, the reason why
Such a resplendent enchantress as she
Should plead with such ardent fervor to be mine,
To only...
So simply...
Just...
Be mine.

The Lament of A Time Once Grand

It was a time, my friend,
Indeed, it was a grand old time;
A time for the searching of souls.
A time for attaining superior goals.
For a time it was a time
We cherished each thought,
Consummated our love
Both in mind and in heart.

And didn't we find,
During this enchanted time,
True enlightenment and peace,
A Gideon's balm, you see,
At last taming our beast.

Yet then did this time ever pass slowly by,
Leaving us lost, alone, and wanting to die,
When we found, suddenly, no time left to cry,
And no time to fathom the reason why.

No time left for the tears,
No room left for the overwhelming fears.
And the whispers that followed,
That sang in our ears
And echoed around us,
Chasing away those good years,
Came soon to burst forth
As screams in the night,
Of horrific design,

Of a maddening plight
That soon brought the evil
Crashing upon us,
The evil so black it extinguished the light,
The light from above, so divinely portentous.

O yes, my friend, indeed, O yes,
That was a time...
That was a grand old time.

Looking Into the Broken Hearts and Mournful Souls of Sad Young Men

Thinking tonight on sad young men,
Their untold memories and broken dreams
And exquisite passions for life, for living
That since have died from emptiness.

Unrequited, consumed in bitterness
And preconceived in desperate hours of loneliness,
These sad young men did watch in silent bereavement
As time so quickly
And so eternally
Passed them by.

All the sad young men,
Searching with a reckless desire,
Indeed, a haunting proclivity,
For a youth they once possessed
But carelessly, senselessly, tossed away.

A youth forever lost in the midst of all human misery;
For seemingly, in contempt of even the best of intentions,
Those best laid plans of centuries past
Are today forever obsolete,
Dismissed completely, with a chilling finality
And sadly laid to rest
With the thousands of other sad young men

Who had, generations before, lived and passed away,
Dying for something...
Finding apparently nothing,
Nothing to show for their lives...
For their living....
For their dying.

A Matter of Time

A time ago,
A not so long a time ago,
I chanced upon a heart...
Twas broken.

I picked it up,
A not so long a time ago,
And cradled it – gently tho,
And fixed it.

But yesterday,
A not so long a time ago,
It stole away softly
And I lay broken.

And now today,
Tho seems a quite long time ago
My spirit drained all out of me.
No more tomorrows
Will I ever know.

Maybe We Can Find a God Somewhere

Originally...
Despite what rumors might dictate...
Contrary to what the demagogues
Would want you to believe...
There was to have been,
Indeed, there had already been,
A set of rules,
Of laws, to be exact,
To lend credence and support
To a way of life, of living
Morally and ethically superior
To anything practiced by us at present;
Superior to anything given us
Or fed to us by example
By those people who know,
Or at least should know,
Better.
That is to say our leaders, fearless and true,
Who were around when the original rules
Had not yet been thrown out,
When they were yet still on the books.

You see, originally...
In the beginning...
There was always a God
And almost always there was his Son;
But again, there were the ten commandments,
And almost always there was the golden rule;
And these were almost always

Taught and practiced in public schools.
For a long time, people who followed
And nurtured the rules,
Indeed, even the rules themselves,
Were held in lofty esteem.

It was, of course,
Impossible to follow these rules perfectly,
But the attainment of perfection
Was not the reason for their existence,
Nor was it ours;
Only that we should attempt it,
This journey toward "enlightenment",
This marching to Pretoria, as it were,
For it was this which was most important;
Failure was unimportant,
Just being on the correct path
Was what mattered.
It was crucial back then
For an honorable life

Today though, they're gone...
They've disappeared...
They've been eradicated
From the memory of man...
Completely.
The God is dead...
The Son is dead...
Their words...
Gone...
Obliterated from the mind of man...
Forever.
There are no rules now,
There are no restrictions;
You may do as you like...
You may hurt whomever you please...
It doesn't matter anymore...
For God exists no longer – He cannot touch you,

You have been saved,
Hallelujah!

But still, you better watch out though,
Watch out for the Man...
The Man with the badge...
The Man with the club and the gun...
Yeah man, watch out.

But hey, if you get caught...
If you slip up somewhere,
Resist him...
Run away...
Hit him even...
And maybe he'll lose his temper...
Then you can sue him for excessive force;
Then you'll be rich!

Hallelujah!!
Praise the Lord!!
For perhaps indeed,
Maybe there is a God after all.

The Meaning of Christmas

One night I saw Santa
Coming down our chimney place.
I tried to tell him of the fire
So's he wouldn't burn his face.
Alas, alack! It was too late;
The flames, their dastardly deed was done!
Yet Santa, finished with his fall,
Exclaimed, "Ho, ho, wasn't that fun?"
Upon which I said to him
"Your fun has just begun!"
As I shot him down with my
Forty-five caliber handgun.
"Thanks," he said. "You've made my day,
But you've also made me dead."

This is what Christmas means to me;
Giving, that is, instead of receiving.
And anytime I can give someone
A ride to another world better than this
I'll happily do it
And enjoy the hell out of it!

Memories

When I was young I had to try,
To break away, I had to try,
To leave the nest, or know I'd die..I'd go

And then I saw my true love's eyes,
Like burning coals, my true love's eyes
And then I heard my Mother's cries...don't go

And as I watched the world go by
I looked and saw our Fathers' die
And I could hear the children cry...don't go

But then my love turned cold as ice,
As white as snow, as cold as ice,
She slipped from me that wintry night...don't go

And when I saw my true love die,
Grow pale, then blue, and then she died,
O I could hear the mountains cry...don't go

But I'd have died a thousand times,
For you, my love, a thousand times,
To give you life I'd give you mine..I'd go

Yet still today the mountains sigh,
The oceans roar, the willows cry,
And in my heart I know that...I'm gone

A Moment in Time

A moment in time, a time not forgotten,
A glistening drop of oil in the memory of man.
Finding our way, the way long forgotten;
Looking for footprints left in the sand;
Time out of time, a time ill-proportioned,
Man against nature, man against man
And this man out of time, this soldier of fortune
Looks to the sky, the stars in his hand.
Wonder of wonders, lights of the sky,
Death when I see the, death walking by
Enlightens my spirit in depth as I cry.
Alone do I stand, sunstorms in my eye,
Alone do I fight, alone do I die,
Alone my bones wither, crumble and lie...
Alone shall I love thee,
Alone knowing why.

A Moment's Remembrance of Time

A time was, a time ago, when beauty did this planet grace...a time when passion flowers in fullness and richness did reign o'er this earth.

But in a moment's haste, a frenzy of lust, the story goes, that in the blink of an eye, just a whisper of time, the rages of vanity enveloped the globe. For they found then an elixir – a miracle drug of the time, that enhanced their fair beauty whilst it also did eliminate all ugliness.

So on this darkest of days did a carnage begin, and upon the nations of the world did mankind himself unleash a plague, a plague most deadly and of vile intent, for its release was financed by the governments of those same nations. The aim of said release was to bring about the brutal slaughter and wholesale annihilation of a people deemed crippled, disfigured or maimed – of any person who in this world of beauty might be found, in a word, ugly.

But something went wrong, as oft' it does when mankind attempts to usurp his nature. When man finds fault with his Creator's original design and aspires to transcend that given perfection. So that when his God said everything is beautiful, that where there is life there can be no ugliness, man, as he is inclined to do, attempted to find a lie there, somewhere, by projecting his own concept of beauty into a world already beautiful. And in so doing he did bring down the wrath of the Heavens, which spewed forth an ugliness of such intense beauty that his mind could not comprehend nor could his soul ever accept.

So now, though centuries have passed, life here on this cold, desolate, barren world attempts to march on. And come each passing dawn, I gaze with fondest memories and sincerest desires out past the desolate streets and crumbling buildings to the fields of my youth, looking to see if somewhere, somehow, a passion flower might yet lift its head and bring once more a patch of beauty into this sea of empty death.

On Happy Days and Empty Nights

Empty cold dark holes in waiting,
Slabs of marble there creating
Caustic markers of days gone by,
Of skinless forms whose children cry
To never see their withered bones
And never hear their soulless moans.

On Mankind, His Soul, and the Understanding of His Desires

A discernible mass of water,
Frozen, and in a cube shaped,
Once removed from its indigenous surroundings
And exposed to the harsher elements
Of this world of mine,
Does, as soft butter when pierced
With a blade of calescent steel,
Subsequently dissipate into,
Then evaporate from my glass.

Upon the execution of this birth of a death,
And while in search of its eventual rebirth,
It maintains an existence
Of incorporeal ambiguity,
Finding itself drifting...
Worthlessly...
Senselessly...
Through the gates of a godforsaken eternity,
Finding itself greeted therein
By the horrific sight and haunting sound
Of one hand clapping.

The subsequent condensation
Of this muck, this mire,
In contention, at this point,
With all other meaningful contingencies,
Forever stains this life of mine
A brilliant, crimson hue,

While simultaneously distorting
The inner sanctions of this,
My mortal soul,
As though my wants, my needs,
Indeed, my every sinful desire,
Were there for all to see,
But only through a glass darkly.

On World War II, an Afterthought

On the blood-slaked shores of Hiroshima
The silence of the dead screamed thru the night
And echoed in the fiery madness of Hell.
But when the bombs fell at Nagasaki
The gods fled in despair,
Leaving behind a timeless void
Of pain,
Lust
And cruelty.

A Passing Thought of Juliet's Passing

Sweet Juliet, my sweet, sweet Juliet,
With thy locks of burnished hair so long
They didst gently caress me
As tenderly, so very tenderly,
You held me in thine arms
And softly, quietly
Didst we behold the coming dawn.

I gazed upon thy misty eyes,
Thy tear-stained countenance
And mine heart didst weep in pain,
For I knew that thee wouldst ne'er reveal to me
The reason for thy sorrow,
The cause of such disdain.

O dearest one, if I'd but only known
That this life of thine
Would in such haste be taken from thee,
That thy heart couldst be so eternally shorn
From thy soul's desire
And that thy pain and mine,
Though so closely intertwined,
Were really miles,
Were so many, many miles...
Apart

Yet on the day thee didst die,
I too alongside thee didst cease to exist.
For twas then that my desire for the spectacle of life
And the joys that it wrought
In their entirety did disappear.

Yes, then didst I love thee, even now do I love thee,
O Juliet, my love for thee is infinite
And groweth ever stronger with each day that passes.
If that I could, I would die
If only to give thy life back to thee,
That life so cruelly taken from thee,

Because thee had always been for me
The truest expression of life itself.
Always, in thy gentle, unassuming nature
Didst thee exhibit the highest ideals
Of love and sincerity,
Never asking for more than what could be given,
But always there to give to me
So much more than I deserved.

O dearest Juliet, why, dear god of mine, oh why
Couldst I ne'er speak these words to thee?
Thou didst mean more to me than life itself,
So, if unknown to thee then,
Then now, please know, please, you have to know...
Thee were for me the finest, the truest love
I couldst ever desire.

For as we wept on that day of thy passing,
It became so clear, so very, very clear,
That whilst thee had been of this earth,
All those whom you had touched – especially myself,
Had been truly bless'd and made beautiful for a time.

God bless thee, sweet Juliet,
I love thee for belong my love, my all,
Indeed, I love thee for simply having been there for me.
And if per chance you may be listening,
Know please that I pray for thee
And that from the depths of mine heart
I wish to God that true happiness in finally thine.

The Plagues of Time
A Trilogy

Part One
The Valley of Lost Innocence

On hither pool of wintry blood,
In ice-cream castles of sunbaked mud,
Lay bodies gored and gods forlorn
And severed heads of unicorns.
And strewn around the castle's walls,
The remnants of death on a lone, pale horse.

Victims of lust, so cruel and sublime,
Consumed by a plague, destroying body and mind;
They yearned for an end to it, lenient and swift,
Too late, they were into it, their souls there adrift.
Ever silently, ever slowly ebbing anon,
With a chilling finality, their life-force now gone.

And the sun, fading weakly, dripped its last golden rays,
Onto the thousands of bodies, twisted, mangled and base
While the maggots came home to a sumptuous delight
Left behind by the vultures, left behind on that night.
And the moon came up singing, it's tune mournful and sad,
It's countenance glistening on the cold, blood-washed sand.

So to all those who mourn for Atlantis this day,
You will find no one listening, there are none to allay
The god-sent destruction of the spirit of man,
That slaughtered their souls
With its plague-ridden hand.

The Plagues of Time
A Trilogy

Part Two
The Bittersweet Reunion of Blood And Tears

Moonlit, midnight massacre,
Blood-washed grains of sand;
The slaughtered children everywhere,
Twas the work of the Devil's hand.

The marauding crusaders tarry forth,
Their paths now turned to dust.
The little bodies and severed limbs
Have become here morsels of food
For nature's timeless, endless lust.

And as they fed upon the children there,
Those crimson, gnarled lumps of flesh torn bare,
Darkness overwhelmed the mighty sun
As God, with a vengeance of furious passion
Unleashed a mighty chaos throughout the land,
With plagues of wanton destruction
Reaching far beyond those blood-washed grains of sand.

And in the madness of those years,
In the land where the blanket of greatest darkness fell,
The marauding crusaders' paths were uncovered;
And it was there where fear was discovered.
For in the darkness of those rat-infested alleys
Did they try so desperately there to hide.

As hard as they tried,
They could not;
He made no allowance for that...
Even as He cried,
He could not...it was their time,
Their time to die.

The Plagues of Time
A Trilogy

A creature deep within the castle bold,
A mighty presence, stark and cold,
Preserves within the massive walls
A cold, cruel knowledge
Of the castle's destined fall.

Unmindful of its coming fate,
Unknowing of this destiny,
Not looking to the east,
Never following the sun,
Indeed, unaware that its day had finally come,
This lofty fortress stood,
Impervious, it believed,
To any weapon made by man,
Made by God or by his Son.

Soon though they found the truth,
With much regret they found it;
A truth with an aftertaste most foul,
A bittersweet lesson of dressing down
And laughing at their God who frowned
At the sodomitic way of life
Chosen by the people of the town
And approved by the King
And then by his crown.

For then did this creature rear its mighty head,
And with its countenance there so fair
This nightmare from Hell didst blacken the sun.
Then following in its wake, disease and famine,
Which on heavenly stallions there didst run
In rapt'rous intent throughout the countryside
As they spread all around them a glorious reign
Of fear, death and utter destruction.
And the scales, as poisoned blood,
Dripped down from off the monster's back,
Each setting off a different plague
When left behind in its harsh and merciless path.

Then finally, as was meant to be,
The castle grand was there no more;
The thick stone's castle walls were gone'
Crumbled...
All to dust.
The castle...
Destroyed from within its walls...
Destroyed from within their minds...
Destroyed from within their souls...
Their souls there...
Destroyed.

Play It Again, Sam

Iridescent clouds of mushrooms
Like slices of phosphorous moonbeams
Destroyed in the inner stratum of this, my life
By the constant swirling and
The overbearing presence of white fluff,
Create in my soul a new life,
A new beginning.
How long I have yearned for this,
This chance, this rebirth.
This overwhelming desire
To be alive.

Pretty Maids in a Row

Twelve beauteous, bounteous, mounds of desire
Rekindle a flame in mine heart,
Ignite my soul into fire.
And life, with such a passionate intoxication
Overwhelms this driving force
Of dying,
Of death,
And the impotence of my station.

But the myriad complexities
Of so contemptuous a thought
Unmask a well guarded secret of herculean proportions,
A voracious tale of perversion that ought
Remain in the bowels of the ancient temples
Of Sodom and Gomorrah.

The Ravages of Time

For five and twenty years has this battle ever raged yet still is found no end in sight – yet even worse is found no desire to end. All around do the bodies lie encrusted in pools of sweet, dried vermillion whilst so busily being attended to by swarms of pernicious vultures, so hungrily, so savagely, so tirelessly relentless in their quest for food.

And I, whilst trampling through these ravaged, war-torn nations, have come across countryside after countryside awash in the angry blood of mighty warriors who died for a cause to fight, and of poor, simple townsfolk who dared fight for a cause to die.

Yet are there also found the bloodied, lifeless and forgotten children;
The tiny, innocent, fragile, soulful children...
Savagely butchered for inconveniently getting in the way of a war nobody wanted,
And for unwittingly frustrating their abominable plans
To continue on with this brutal, necessary apocalypse.
Necessary...
     To kill all so as to kill no more;
               Necessary...
               To die for all so as to die no more.

O the children...
     O the woe-begotten children!
          To God be their salvation
               And from God may we His mercy obtain.

Serendipity in Motion

Eternity in motion...
Revolution in progress...
Infinity forever lost...
Forever yearning a past...
                    A future...
                              A purpose.
Forever yearning an end...
Sometime...
          Somewhere...
                    Somehow...
                              Some day;
Some day an end to it.
And then perhaps by chance
The death of it.
A death to bring forth a new life...
A new life to start once more...
Anew.

A Simple Act

Simply living, hardly dying,
Never knowing, hardly trying,
Finding Paradise in a grain of sand,
There you are, please take my hand.
Could you all but know, my love
What futures are in store for us?
All of the best,
Some of the worst, and if we are lucky
We might make it first.
But if we don't, if maybe we can't,
We'll know we had tried...
Tried so simply just to die.

Soft Now, the Ever Haunting Resonance of Silence

A song of silence...
An eerie haunting silence...
A song for the open soul...
A soul once opened,
Now closed.
A soul once full of life
Now dying...
Now dead.

And from the grave
The screams of horror...
Of evil...
Of Satan...
Rise to touch the ears of God
Who smiles...
Who laughs...
Who fills this void of silence
With life...
With music...
With pangs of joy...
Forever.

A Song for the Open Soul

Somewhere...
Somewhere from a place beyond
She calls to me
With whispers soft of promises sweet
And faint, lilting strains of mystical treats.

So many times I'd heard this though,
This chorus of lies,
These words of deceit.
And any pleasures they may once had brought forth
Have become now hollow and sweet
Having since hardened my heart
Imto a life bittersweet.

Thus devoid of all passion
And stripped of all caring
I travel the highways of my pain-ridden soul
Still seeking undauntedly some elusive goal;
Still searching for answers to questions unknown,
And still knowing from somewhere...
From some place beyond me,
She'll call yet again,
Her whispers still soft,
Her promises still sweet.
And I'll find myself once more
Listening to the faint, lilting strains
Of her magical, mystical treats.

But now, when she does call again,
My renewed strength and wisdom
Will protect me from her lies.

Tears for the Lost Souls

We are souls in the wind
With no beginning and no end;
Who were born out of time,
Without reason, without rhyme,
And we're dying now
To find our way
To Heaven.

We were lost, long ago,
Aborted once so long ago;
Like seeds that never grew,
Never blossomed
Never knew.
Still we're dying now
To find our way to Heaven.

We were life gone awry,
Products of lust,
Destined to die.
But our souls will linger on,
Ever present, never gone;
And we will die no more,
Just couldn't find our way
To Heaven.

Tell Me Mr. Vagabond Man

Tell me Mr. Vagabond Man,
Tell me won't you please,
How long you've been in search for life,
You with your sword of Damocles?
Do you have a destination?
Do you know which road to take,
Or do you let the roads take you
On journeys many have yet to take?
Journeys far beyond the untamed wilds
Or far across the raging seas
Mr. Vagabond man tell me,
Tell me, won't you please,
Where're you're bound,
From whence did you come,
How much farther your quest for peace?
Please, Mr. Vagabond man,
Won't you answer, won't you please?
Mr. Vagabond man...
Please.

This Enemy Mine

I, with my tortured memories,
Do sail along the turbulent shores
Of a violent sea of crimson blood,
While riding along on this cold and rusty carousel
Of this, my life.
I travel the effervescent sea of my obsession here
Which I find then flows
Into a calm and bitter tasting pool
Of sweet, sweet death.
I pause there briefly, for the most time allotted me
To search for faces friendly,
To look for lost loves,
Finding there none to see;
Is a lonely, sad and piteous journey,
One made quite soon by all,
Closing ears to dying spirits...
                    Crying souls...
                        Unloved hearts

And as I sail along the troubled shores
Of this misty sea of blackened blood,
I follow with fiercest need the music of my life
As this carousel of time
Weaves intricate designs and celestial desires
Throughout this ephemeral spiritual being
I dare not claim as mine own.
However, this constant stepping on and stepping off
This carousel bound for Hell
Gives leave to an endless, careless desire to search...

To search for an exit...
        For a door...
             For a life...
                  For something...
                        Something better.

And yet there is a splendor during this time,
This time beyond all time,
That remains imbedded and implanted
Within the innermost recesses
Of my dark, insidious mind,
And that, God forgive me,
I will not...
Nay, I cannot release!
             Not from here...
                Not from this soul...
                    This spirit...
                        This enemy mine.

The Thoughts and Ruminations
of Wile E. Coyote

The music of my heart, twisted, gnarled and broken,
Cries bitterly in the night,
Sending forth sad refrains of unkempt promises, empty dreams
And gratuitous reminders
That life has only just begun.

This deafening cacophony of sounding joy, so to speak
Rings incessantly throughout my soul,
Leaving no time at all for even a hint
Of acquiescent rebellion on my part,
Even should I desire.

Yet the masochistic pleasures derived
From everlasting memories of failures,
Both past and present,
Keep me awash in painful reflection,
So as each time to assure me –
As though with the pride of nations –
That after each hellish descent that is surely coming,
I will most regrettably still be alive
And will most aggrievedly find,
That once again,
It will be time to go on.

A Time of Madness

It was a night like any other – cold, bleak and dreary and the time that night passed none too quickly. Through the trees I could see the moon winding its way across the midnight sky with such reluctance, so much resistance as it slowly edged its way into morning while at the same time, fighting with every ounce of strength it possessed to somehow, in some way, hold back the dawn.

It was comforting to me to observe such a struggle, indeed, almost a fight for survival, whilst being tossed about in this struggle of mine own. It had always been to me to be a drab, boring inconsequential life, utterly filled with tedious familiarities. For some reason I had always been happier, most comfortable, when I had to fight, to struggle my way through my own existence, so that indeed, I was not merely existing but rather, in a very active role, living!

But this, by my father's gods! This had become more devastating then I might ever have thought. Our entire journey, the battles thus far, the wanton physical abuse of both man and beast had been unseen, unprepared for and incomprehensively lethal. Amazingly, the number of warriors on each side had been maintained at an equal number, both sides having been overwhelmed by an outside force – a force into which I and my men had been lured – a snare which forced us to play as pawns in some sort of twisted game of murder and mayhem.

Thus we were forced to continue – even against our desire to do so – as the madness reached out, where, in the veil of that darkness, it tore away at our minds and overwhelmed in the process that very real desire. For at that moment there was given no allowance for resistance, for refutation, for surrender. Finally there was given no permission to, in some way, escape this bloodbath.

It was then, at that time, this became here a place to come no longer to fight great battles but rather was it now a place to come to die meaningless deaths. A place where death had become so removed from the old rugged cross, that the only way to defeat this most monstrous evil and keep it from possessing our very life-force was to allow death to consume our wretched souls, as it was only then, in those final hours of this god-forsaken madness did we dare to watch as the subsequent light consumed this demon into an oblivion of hell. It was then as we watched that we knew we'd been saved... that we were once more truly alive.

To Dawn, My Wife, My All

O Dawn, my love, my truest love,
Thou art the keeper of mine heart,
The protector of my soul;
And throughout this love we have shared
Thee has been my dearest, my best,
Indeed, my only true friend.
And all that thee has done for me this day
Has ever more secured this love,
Has ever so strengthened this bond,
Has ever more assured me that our love is true.

From my heart to thine
I give thee eternal thanks,
For indeed, had thou never been there for me
In those times of greatest need,
Then most truly I would never have survived
The tumult, the anguish, the aloneness
That would forever have been mine.

And in that moment of deepest despair
Would my soul have truly perished.
Dawn, with thy love thee hast blest me
Far greater than words could e'er attest,
And so very far beyond any ability I might possess
To return such an endearment.
So if ever I have come short
Of expressing my true feelings for thee,
Let me tell thee now I do so passionately love thee;

So completely have I loved thee
That I burn with everlasting pride and glory
To have been wed to thee all these years.

And the children we have raised together
Have truly been pearls of great worth;
And to have them in my life
Does indeed honor me so
and goes even further to elevate thee in my life.
So Dawn, always remember that, come what may,
Thou wilt forever be of mine heart,
Thou wilt forever be of my soul,
And to my dying day
Thy name wilt forever be on my tongue.
Stay well, my wife.
Stay well and God Speed, my cherished one.

The True Ugliness of a Beauty Most False

It was once a mystical, magical land,
A land of wondrous delights;
A land past the lemonade stands
And far beyond the last crackerjack band;
A place where even the Good Ship itself could not land.

However, the brilliant opulence of this hamlet
Has finally been corroded by the sinister
Yet inevitable erosion of time;
And this sensual, maddening, blissful land
That once reigned most stately
With a glorious splendor there so grand,
Has here at last become a dark, bitter cold
And yet mysteriously resplendent retreat –
A Glory Hole, in kind – there to greet
A people, whose final true desire is a bittersweet
End, planned most discreet.

Because although for glorious sex and fun,
It was once the grandest place to come,
And tho forever seemed a place
Where only fair beauty would ever grace,
Is now a strife-torn, plague-ridden land
Overrun with pestilence, fire and flood,
Overcome with pollution, sewage and rot,
And finally consumed by the death and destruction
Of all that was beautiful...
Or at least, what was beauty in thought.

Untitled

Lord of my soul, light of my life
Lifts me out of my anguish,
Leads me away from my strife.
O wondrous Savior, o Spirit divine,
As You are with me I shall be Thine,
Allowing our bodies, our souls
And our hearts to thus intertwine.

What Fate the Moon?

As the bombs come falling,
Castles crumble in the wind;
Like little toy soldiers
And the games we used to play
But never win

Like the sands passing through an hourglass
Is the ice as it melts in my glass,
Both, the sound of nothing they make
As angels dance upon on the grass
While my true love's maidenhead
I prepare to take.

Roll away, roll away,
Blood upon the moon;
Pegasus, my one, my own,
How can it be...too soon,
Blood upon the moon...
The moon.

Lithesome child, so long forgotten,
High up on a mountain's crevice,
Old, withered, cracked and dry;
Take heed my friend and worry not,
The time is come, our time to die.

So take my hand and walk with me
And we together both shall be
The reason for the blood upon the moon...
The reason...
Why.

What Would He Say?

Caught in the passionate moments and maddening desires
To kill a mockingbird
Winging softly, swiftly through the midnight sky
Brings me to a sudden fierce absolution
Of life and death;
And just as sudden
An absolute need to cry...
To pause for tears,
Tears for grief and tears for sorrow;
To pause for a moment, wond'ring why.
A time out, a second please!
A time to determine
If whether for a time
This is right,
Or at least...
Okay.

What would He say,
Indeed, what will He say,
At that time...
On that day,
When the last church bell clangs away
As it tolls for you and me
In its back and forth decisive sway?
What will He finally have to say
When the blood drips off the moon
And the stone has rolled away?
Will there be anything more, then,
Left to say?

Or perhaps we'll just be gone...
In the flash of that moment,
Gone away...
As the mockingbird, in festive spirit,
Takes the day
And flies...
Flies away.

Why I Write

In those early days,
In those days when the darkness
First made itself known to me...
I remember a change overtaking me;
An emptiness, a hollow despair,
And then a terrible, sudden inadequacy
Of being me...
Of just being me.

When only days, weeks before
I had been so near to perfect –
At least as close to what was considered perfect
At the time.
Another birthday had come and gone
When suddenly my true love
Was struck with cancer
And was soon taken from me.
And then, at 31, my youth seemed all spent,
and suddenly, alone was I now...
Alone...facing this pain.

That was the hardest part,
The aloneness of it all;
The inability to find anyone
Comfortable enough to open
Their heart, soul and ear.
For someone who would
Sit for any length of time
And provide the needed
Shoulder to cry on.

O if only I could have spoken
Of the ever increasing pain haunting me
Before it overwhelmed me in its entirety.
Instead I said nothing,
Just suffered in silence.
Just leaving them wondering –
And I knew they were wondering –
"What the bejeezes has got into that boy?
He cries at the drop of a hat,
He doesn't talk to anyone anymore,
Has he said anything to you?"

Eventually I started looking for death,
A way out – tho not by my hands.
I would cross the streets when lights were green
But not look both ways, allowing anyone to hit me
Should they run a red light.

While making sure no trains were coming
I would sometimes jump onto the subway tracks looking for money,
When I spotted one coming I would climb out,
Hoping that one day I might slip
So as to finally be rid of my pain;
Fortunately this did not happen.

It was after 4 years of this descent into hell
When I started writing.
It was a time when I started hearing voices,
Voices on top of everything else.
Voices shouting from out of nowhere,
Voices calling out my name -
Nothing else, just my name...
And then something, I don't know what,
A message from God, for all I know,
Told me to write, just start writing.

Now I'm not a writer, never was,
But still I set out writing...and writing...
And by God if I wasn't half-way through

With an epic poem that came from I know not where
when suddenly I looked up, listened...
Then realized, the voices were gone!
Not that they never came back - they did,
In moments of darkness and solitude
They would come back, but while I wrote
I found I could keep them at bay.
I also learned that the more I wrote
The more I was able to lift myself from,
Or at least keep myself from sinking deeper
Into the pit of despair in which I had fallen
So many years ago.

I learned soon enough, though,
It was not a cure.
For there were many days when I couldn't write,
Days when nothing came to me.
And then there were the nights...
Always there would come those
Long, lonely, dark and oppressive nights
That seemed to set me back 5 days worth of writing.
But still it was something...
A glimmer of light, of hope,
Finally making its way into this life where
For years there had been only darkness.

And that is the story behind
What got me started writing.
What keeps me writing now, though,
Now that I am rarely besieged by the demons of yore
And no longer hearing the voices,
Is simply because it's fun.
The challenge of finding new uses for old words
And new stories using untried plot-lines;
Is what writers live for,
What they would die for,
And what I constantly search for!

You Know, I Had a Thought

How odd, I thought,
To find myself alone again,
Sitting here to think once more about the
Variations on the singular theme of love and death...
To say, that is,
Loving to die,
And dying to love.
Music as this drifts throughout my conscious mind
And creates there, amidst all the other turmoils,
A web of altruistic and intrinsic desires...
The desires of both tearing me asunder.
Thus is born a psyche of both shadow and light,
Substance and air,
Love and hate,
Life and death.

To find somewhere a combination of these
Most true to myself...
Most true to my spirit...
Yet also least lethal to my soul's desires,
Gives rise to the quiet need of a solid foundation
Upon which to lay bare my deciduous being
And then offer up my naked soul
To the love and subsequent pain
Of this lustful quest I desire.

Is a most glorious quest though,
A quest of sparkling, joyous innocence;

And yet, soon, possibly innocence lost.
For it is also a battle of mortal wits...
Of sinful desires and deviant, worldly delights.
And you will find the path most easily taken
To be inherently selfish,
Quite unmindful of the feelings
Or of the pain inflicted on others
Just so one might experience those sensuous delights.

And then realize also, that soon, after a time,
The quest will be over and then you will find
The Holy Grail to still be elusively out there,
Somewhere...
            Waiting to be found.

And then will come the pain...
The pain amidst the realization...
The realization that nothing will ever be the same...
The realization of wasted years...
Wasted, with nothing to show for them,
Nothing of any consequence to be sure.

No true love to share the pain,
No God out there to perhaps explain,
No one really to blame;
No one that is, except yourself...
None finally...
But yourself.

And then come the tears,
The tears for the unsaved...
                        The unloved...
                    The lost...
                        Soul.
The soul once more lost,
Finding itself once again loving to die...

Or maybe, perhaps still in this lifetime...
Maybe, with just a little luck,
Once again, dying to love.
I don't know...
It was just a thought.

Printed in the United States
by Baker & Taylor Publisher Services